LITTLE BIG BOOK
PLUS

Table of Contents

Meet
Margaret Miller

The children in Margaret Miller's books are all friends of hers. Ms. Miller says, "Taking photographs teaches you to see in a special way. I especially love photographing children."

MY FIVE SENSES

BY MARGARET MILLER

HOUGHTON MIFFLIN COMPANY

BOSTON

ATLANTA   DALLAS   GENEVA, ILLINOIS   PALO ALTO   PRINCETON

For my mother,
who always encouraged me to see

AUTHOR'S ACKNOWLEDGMENTS
My special thanks to the children in this book:
Miranda Berman, Annie Bernard, Rafael Espaillat,
Max and Gus Halper, Gideon Jacobs, and Morgan
Means.
—M.M.

Acknowledgments

For each of the selections listed below, grateful acknowledgment is made for permission to excerpt and/or reprint original or copyrighted material, as follows:

Text

1 *My Five Senses,* by Margaret Miller. Copyright © 1994 by Margaret Miller. Reprinted by permission of Simon & Schuster Books for Young Readers, Simon & Schuster Children's Publishing Division. **25** "Ayii, Ayii, Ayii," from *Songs of The Dream People: Chants and Images from the Indians and Eskimos of North America.* Edited by James Houston. Copyright © 1972 by James Houston. Reprinted by permission of the author. **28** "Look Closely," from *Sense Suspense: A Guessing Game for the Five Senses,* written and illustrated by Bruce McMillan. Copyright © 1994 by Bruce McMillan. Reprinted by permission of Scholastic, Inc.

Illustrations

25–27 Maureen Zimdars.

Photography

i Banta Digital Group. **ii** Courtesy of Margaret Miller (tl, tr, bl); Banta Digital Group (background).

Houghton Mifflin Edition, 1996
Copyright © 1996 by Houghton Mifflin Company. All rights reserved.

Printed in the U.S.A.

ISBN 0-395-73151-8

6789-B-98 97 96

I have two eyes, a nose,

a mouth, two ears, and two hands.

With my eyes I see myself,

my shadow,

my dog,

and my city.

With my nose I smell popcorn,

a horse,

flowers,

and garbage.

With my mouth I taste watermelon,

the ocean,

medicine,

and ice cream.

With my ears I hear my baby brother,

a fire engine,

my piano,

and whispered secrets.

With my hands I feel finger paints,

sand,

water,

and a rabbit.

With our five senses, we enjoy our world.

AYII, AYII, AYII

an Inuit chant

Ayii, ayii, ayii,
My arms, they wave high in the air,
My hands, they flutter behind my back,
They wave above my head
Like the wings of a bird.

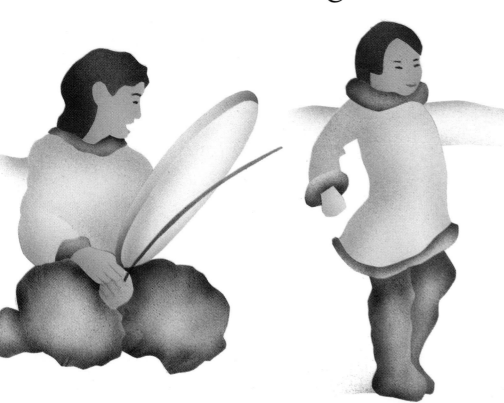

Let me move my feet.
Let me dance.
Let me shrug my shoulders.
Let me shake my body.

Let me crouch down.
My arms, let me fold them.
Let me hold my hands under my chin.

translated by James Houston

Look Closely

by Bruce McMillan

SENSE SUSPENSE
A GUESSING GAME FOR THE FIVE SENSES
Bruce McMillan

English		Español
I see		Yo veo (YO VAY•o)
I touch	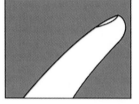	Yo toco (YO TOE•co)
I smell	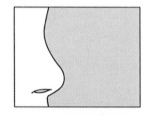	Yo huelo (YO WELL•o)
I taste	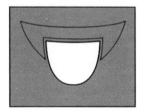	Yo saboreo (YO sah•bor•RAY•o)
I hear		Yo oigo (YO OY•go)

28

Can you guess what these things are?

1

2

3

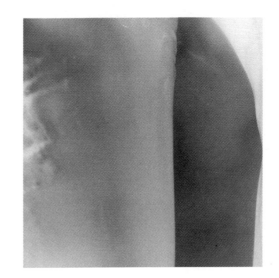

4

Here are the same things.
Are you surprised?

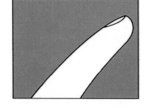

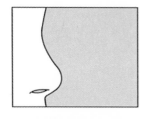

1

3

2

4